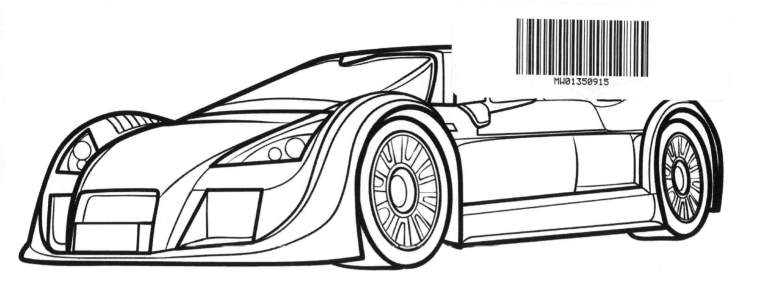

THE BOOK
   BELONGS TO:

_____

_____

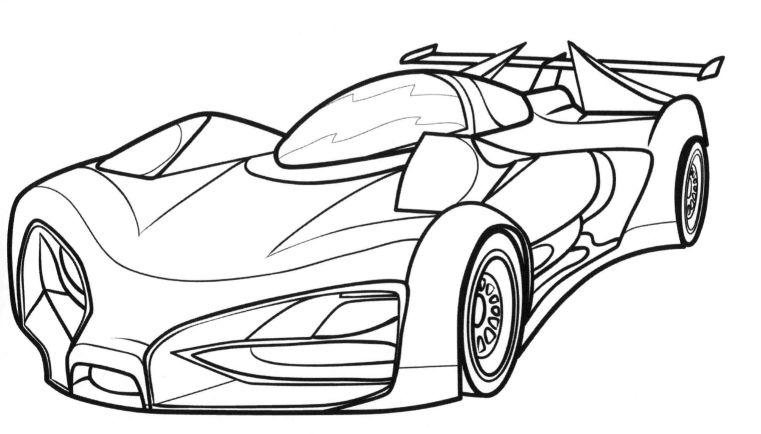

Copyright © 2023 Jam Books. All rights reserved.

No part of this book may be reproduced, distributed, or transmitted in any form or by any means, including photocopying, recording, or other electronic or mechanical
methods, without the prior written permission of the publisher

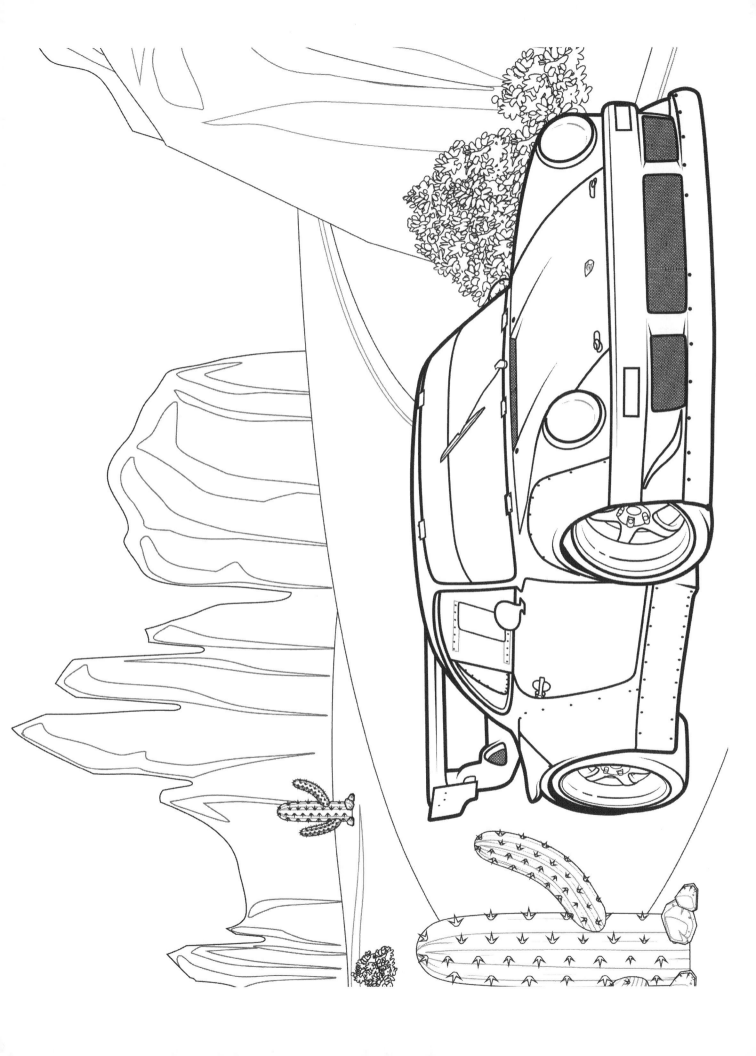

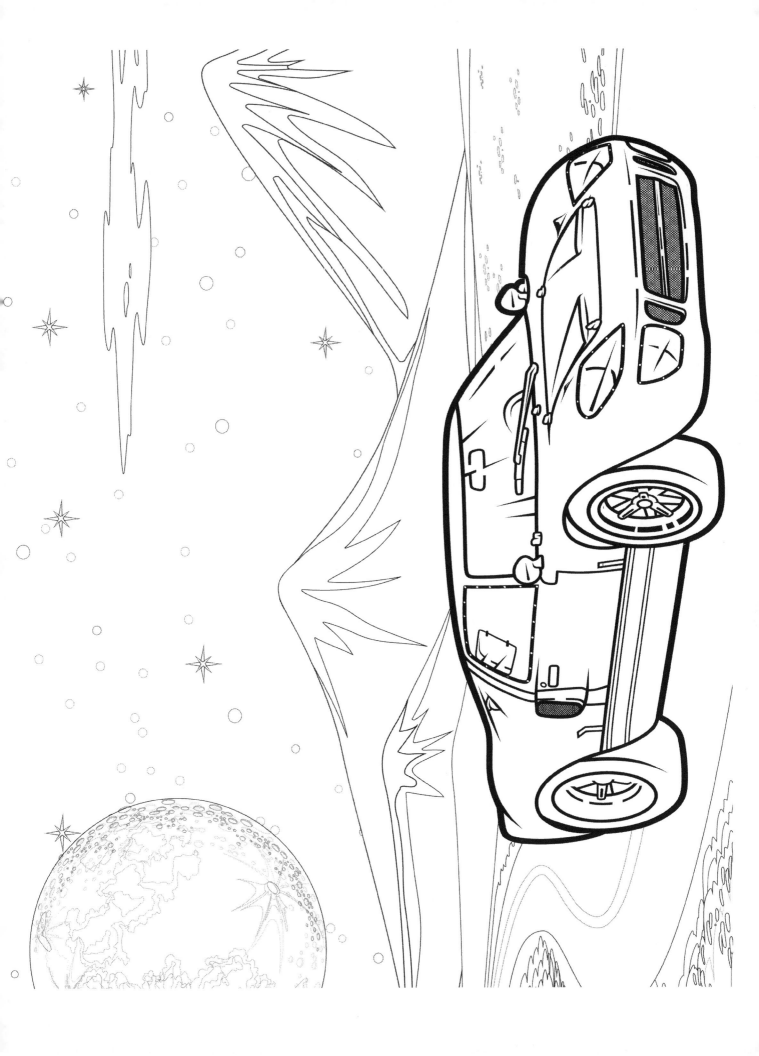

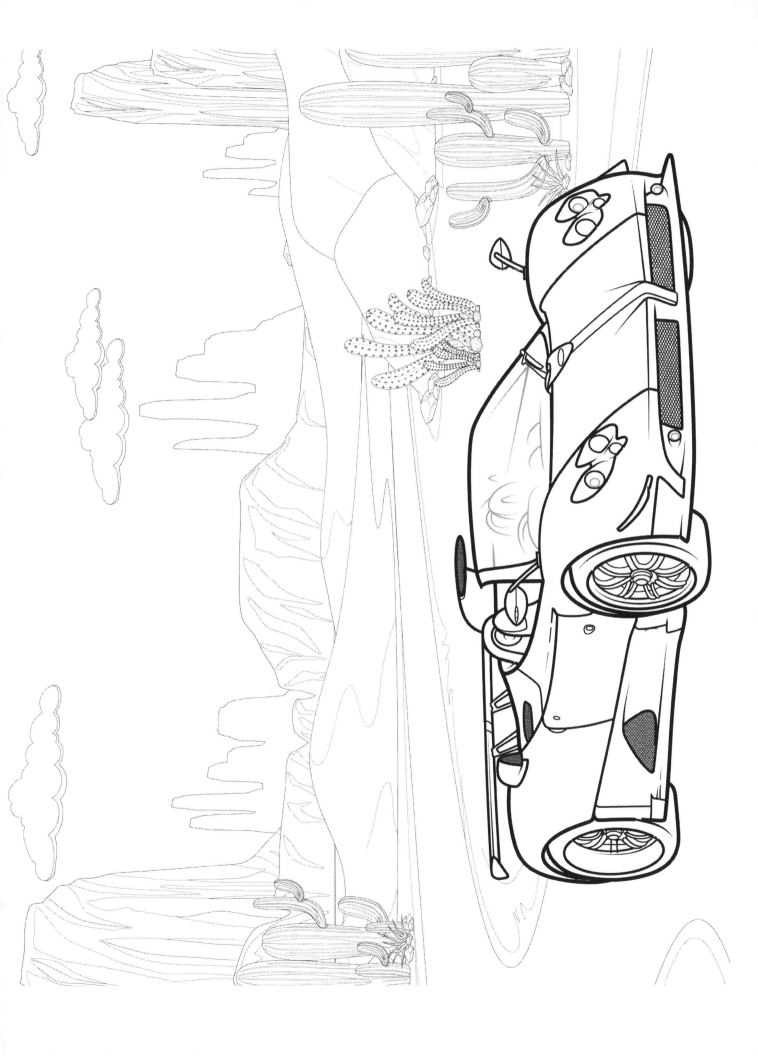

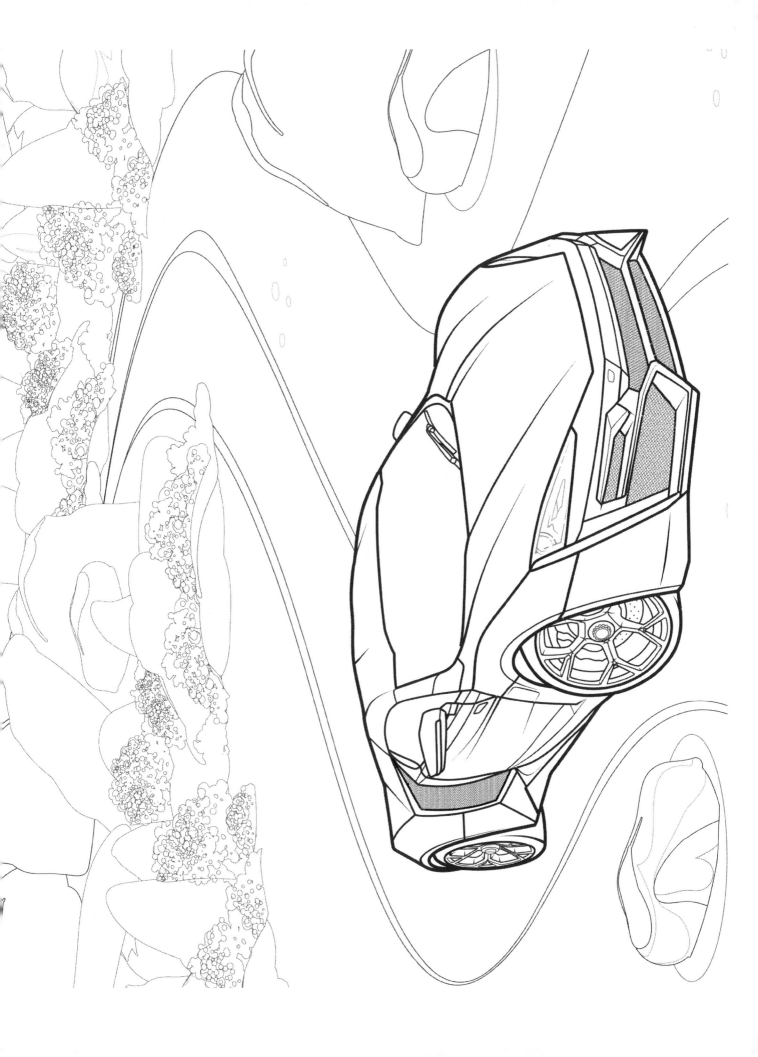

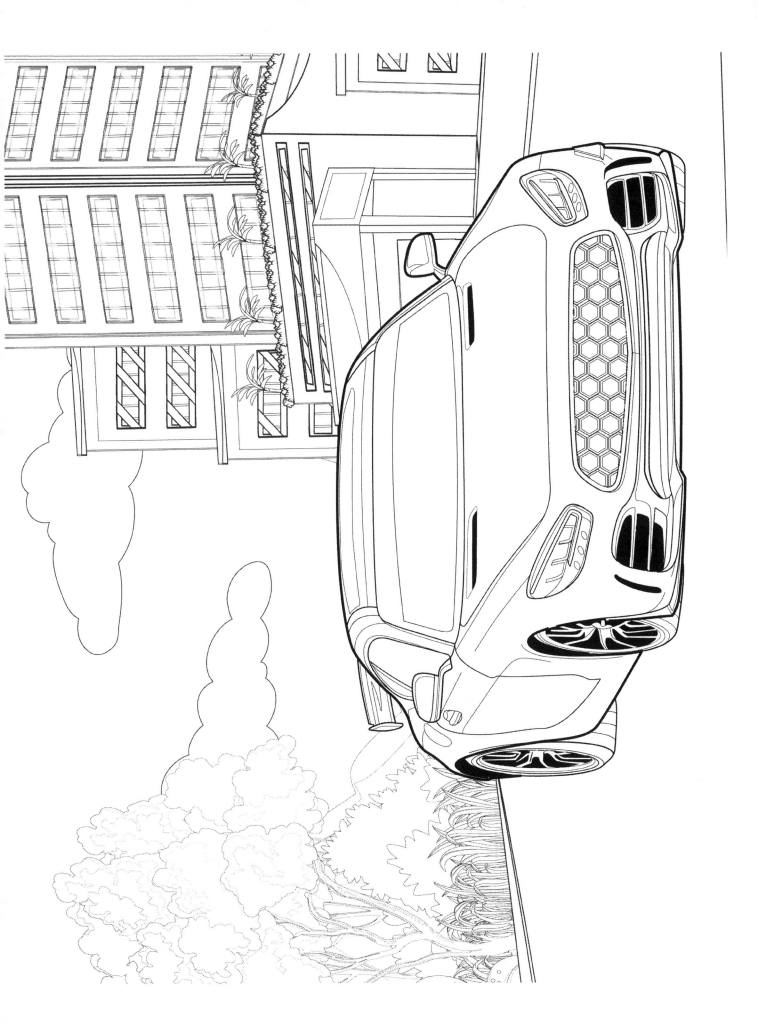

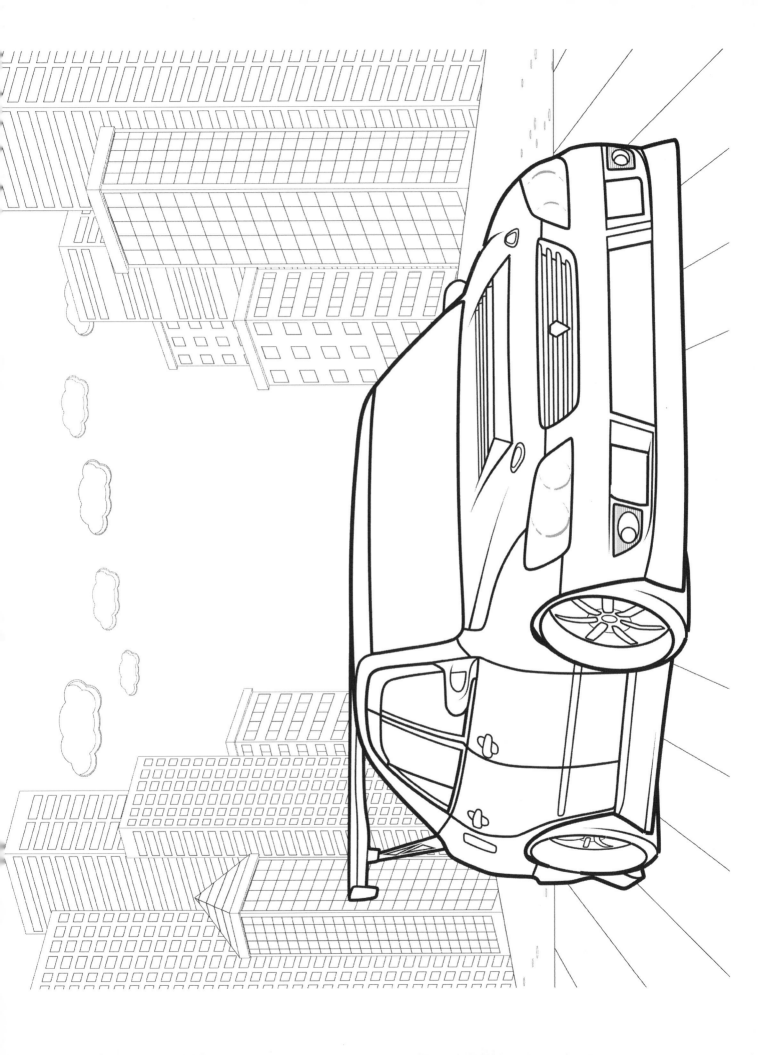

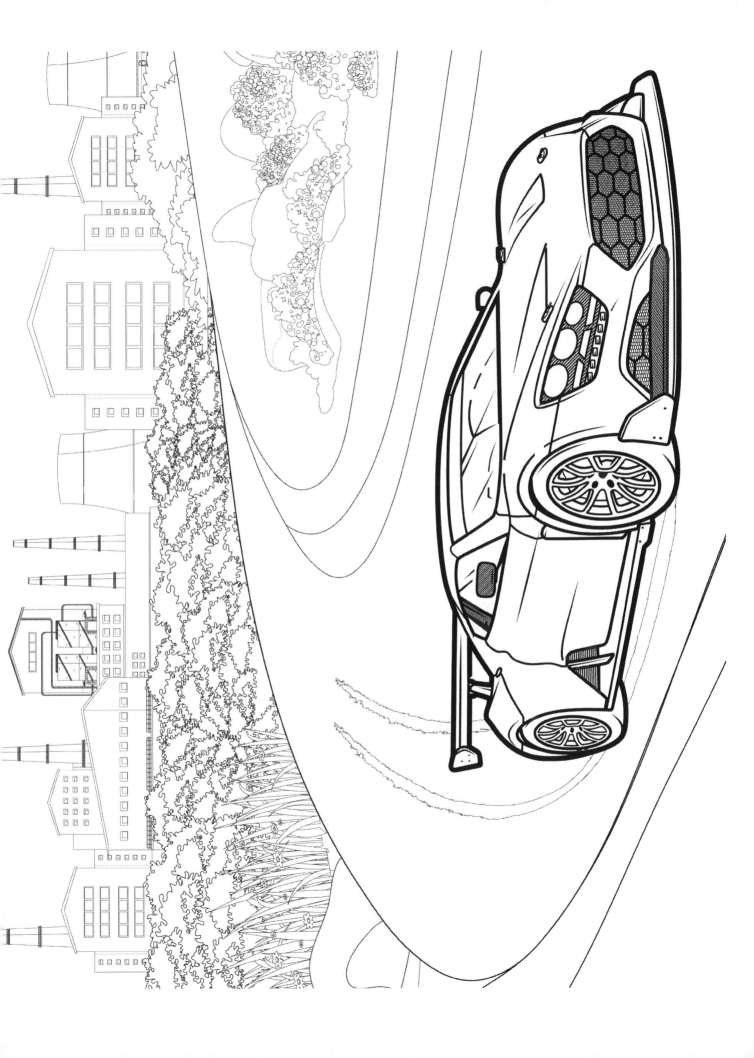

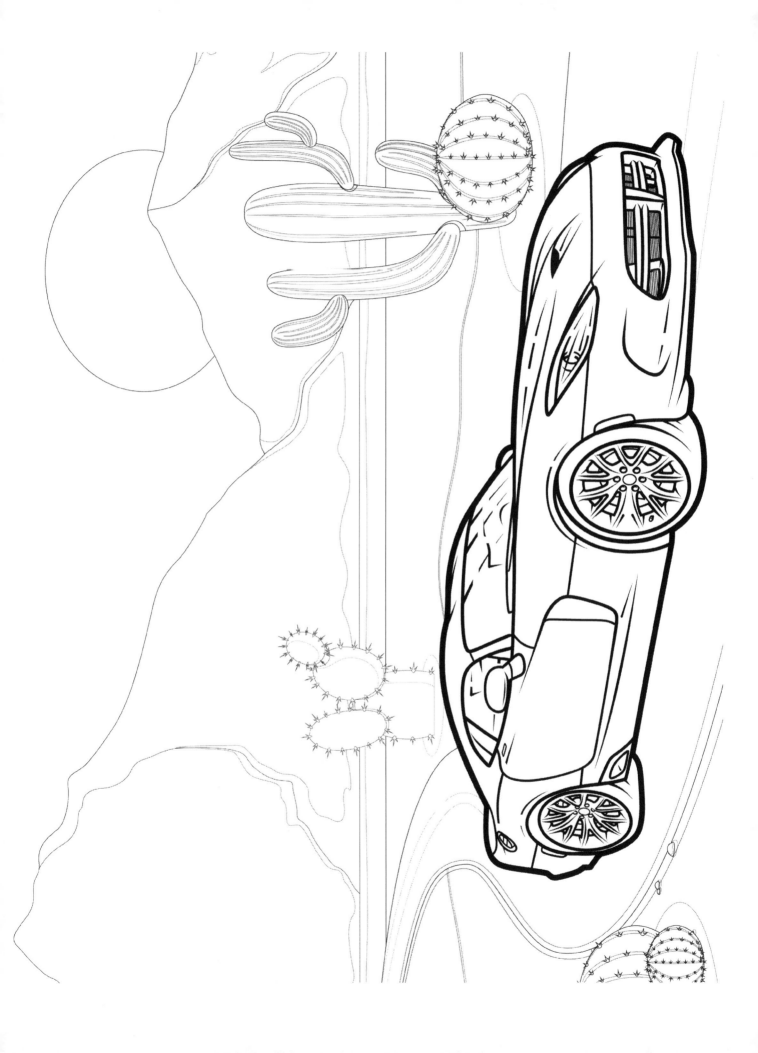

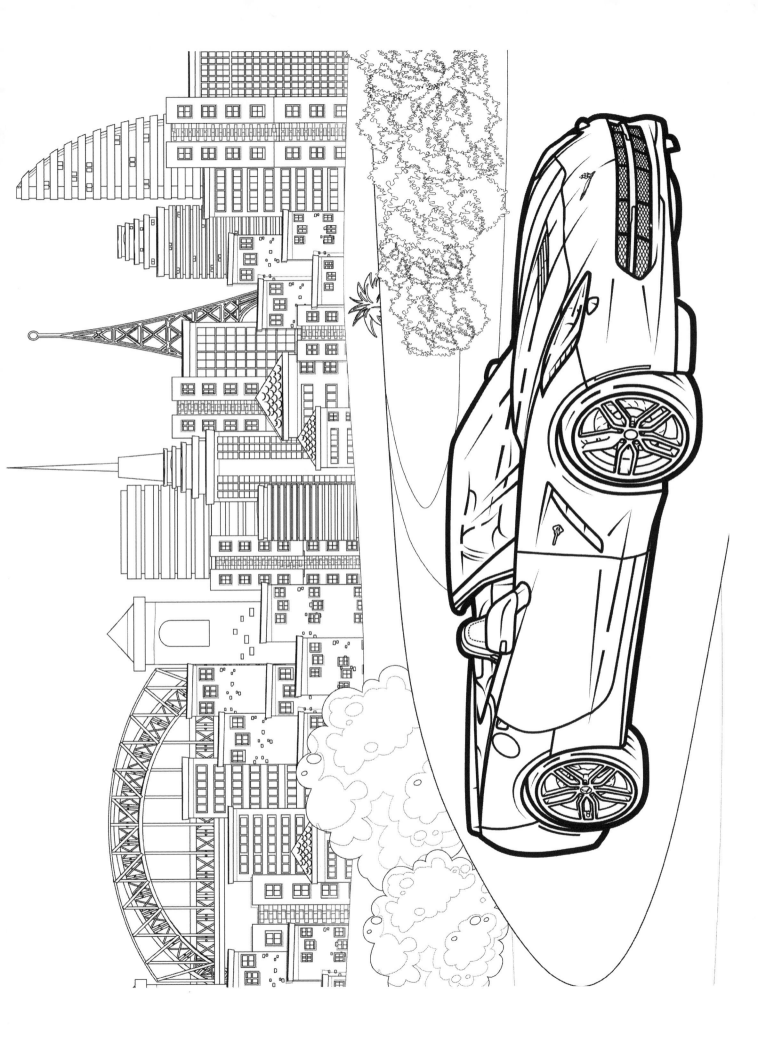

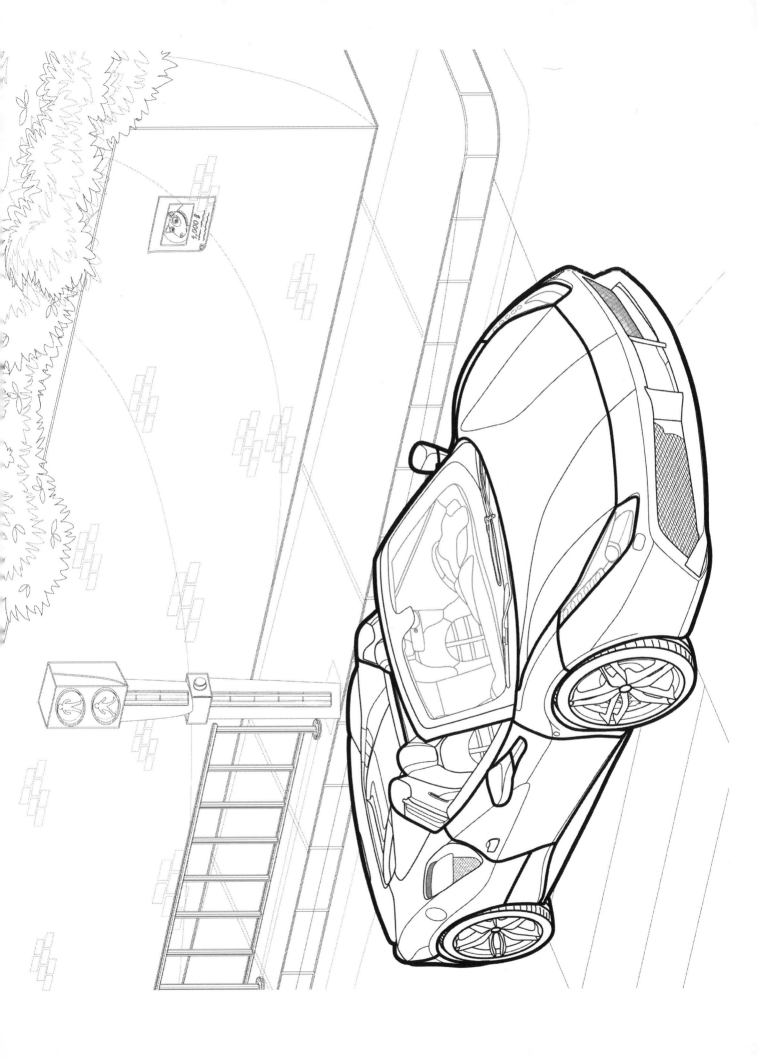

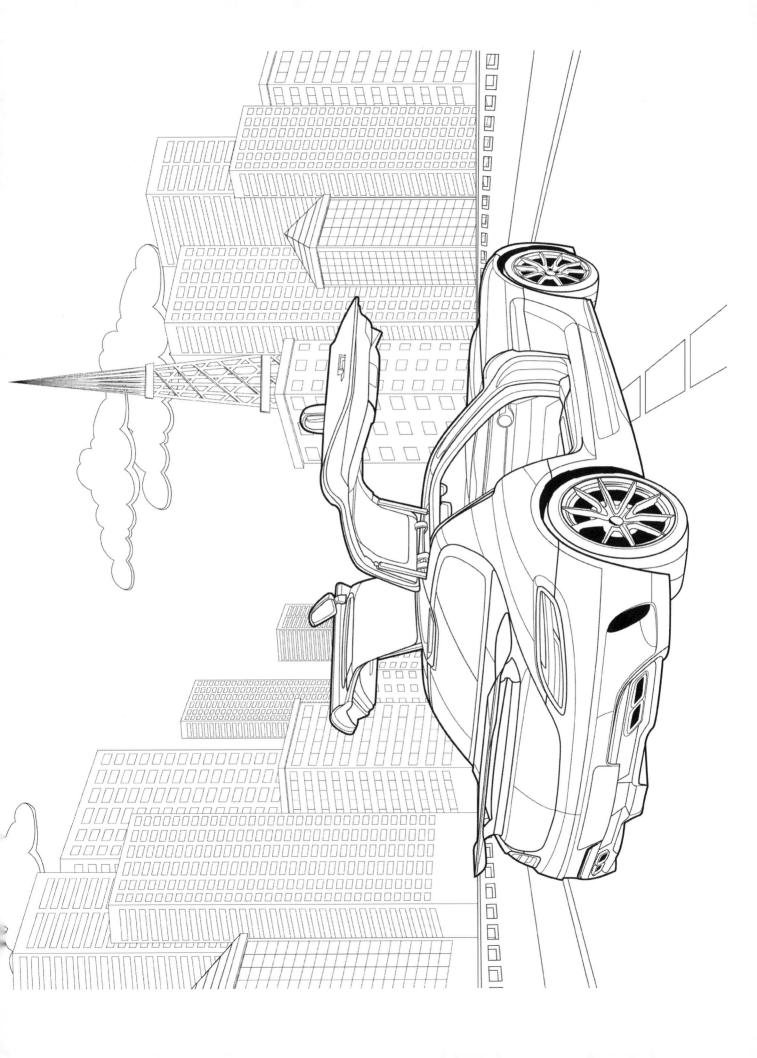

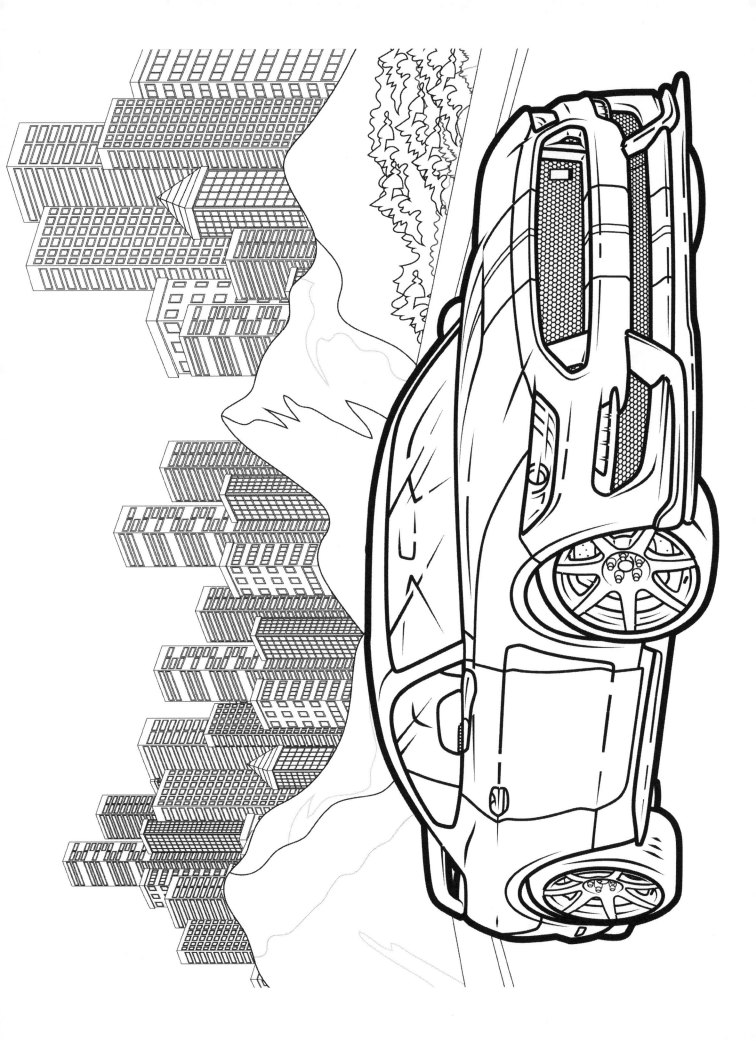

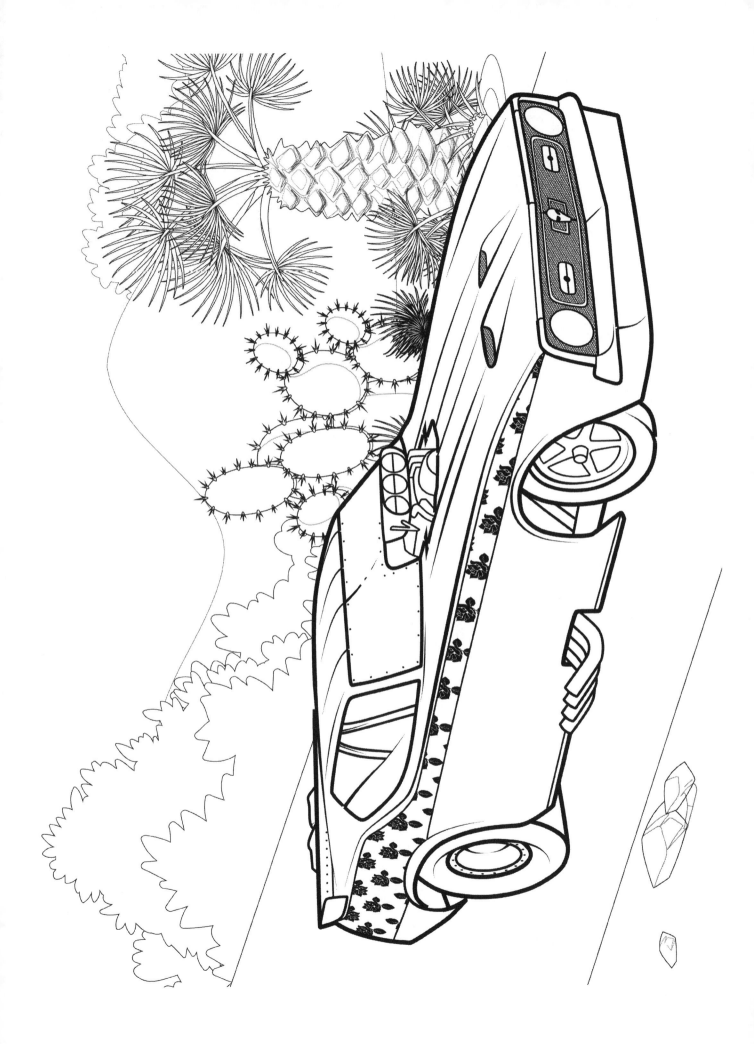

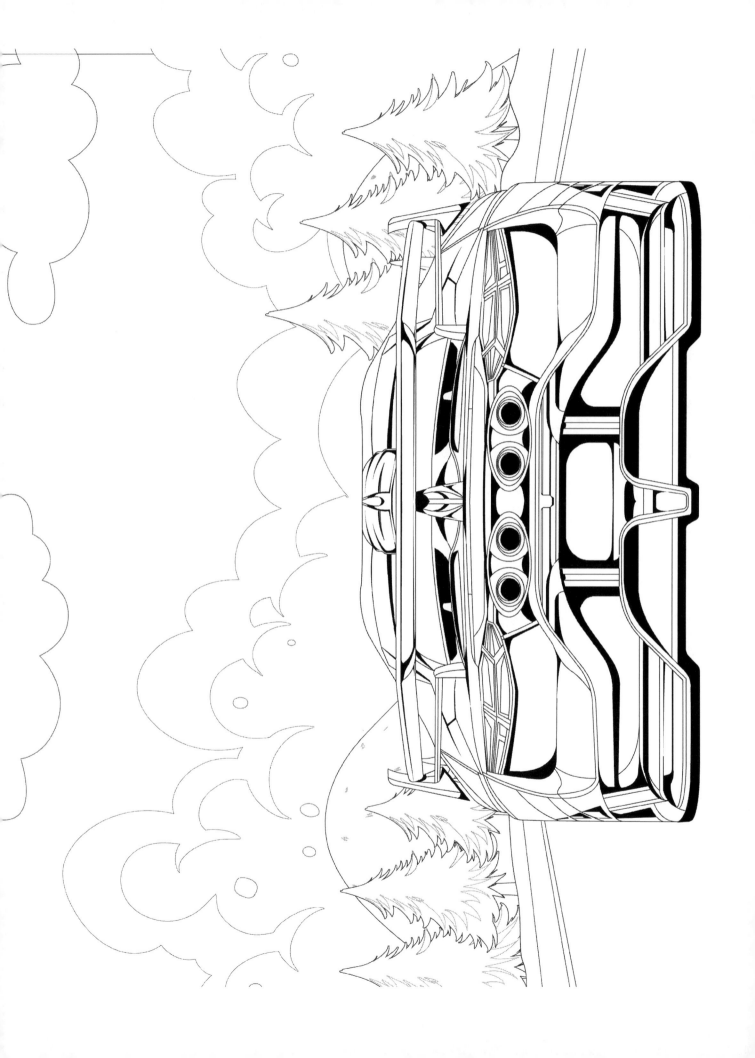

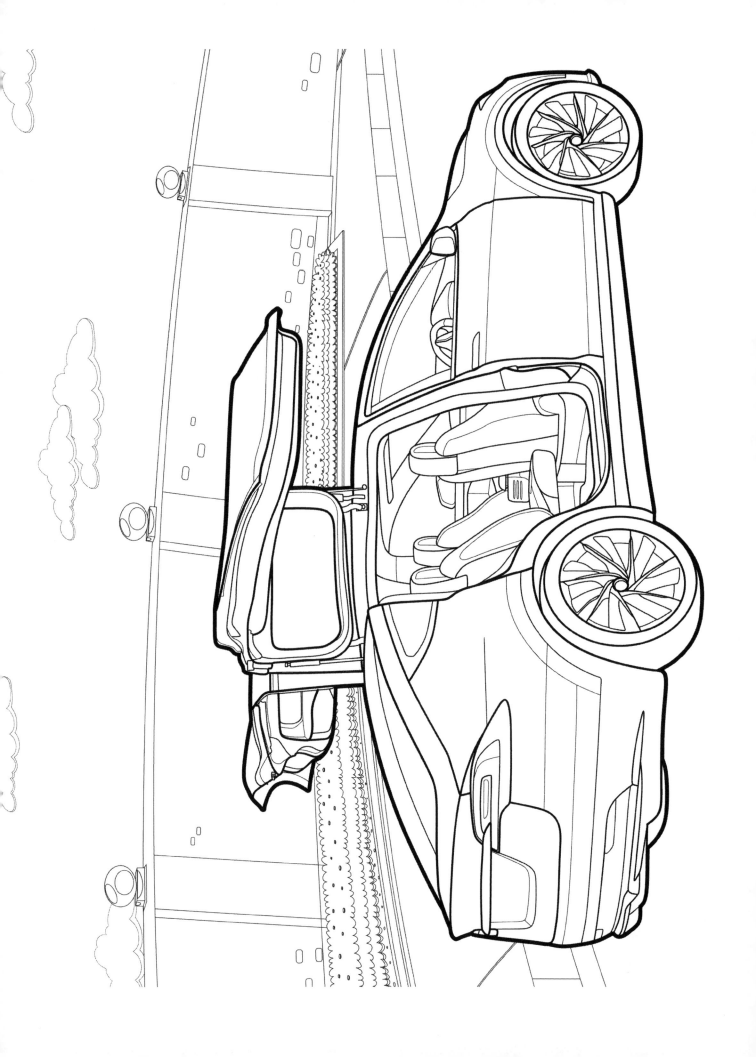

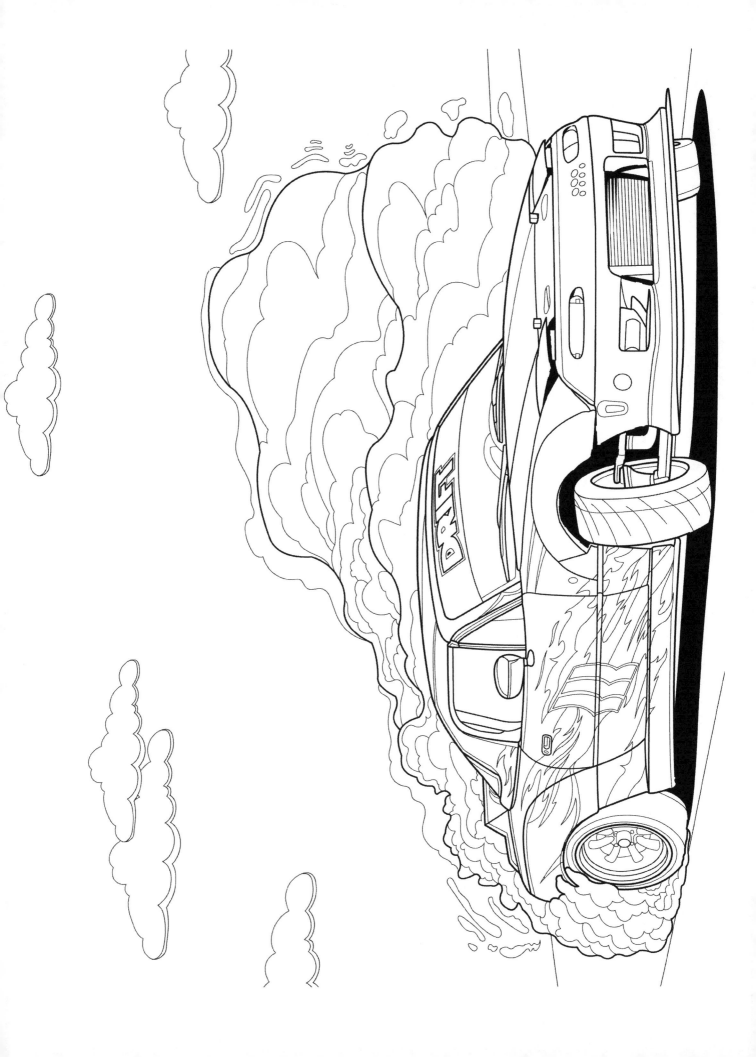

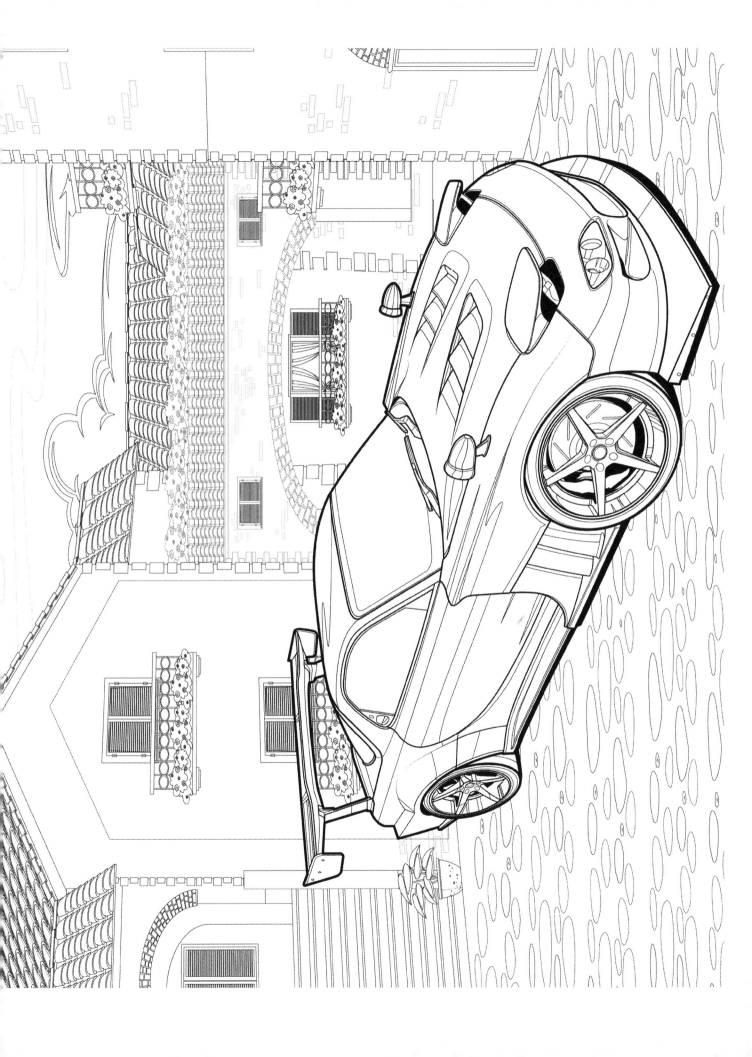

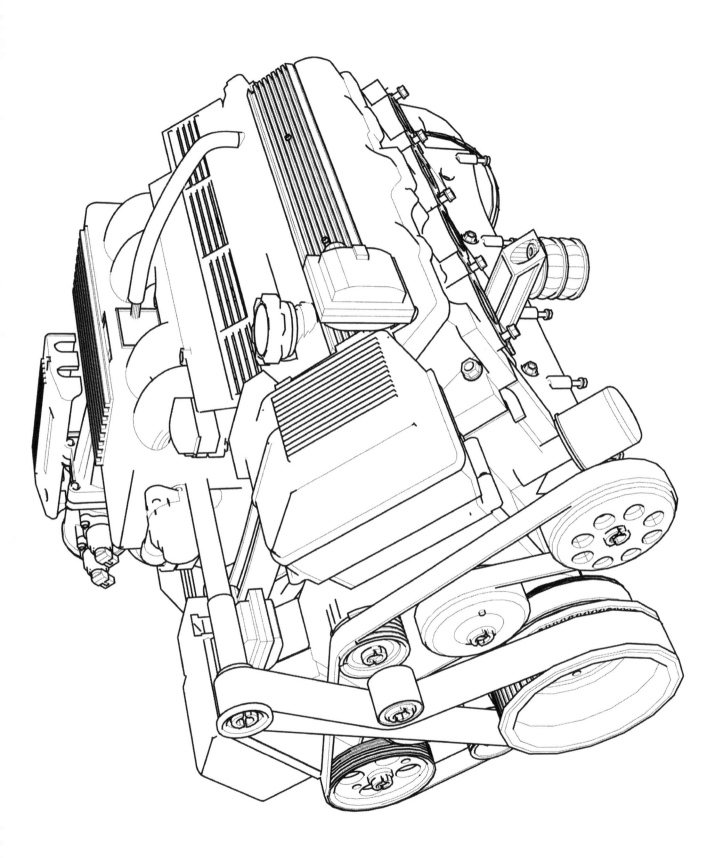

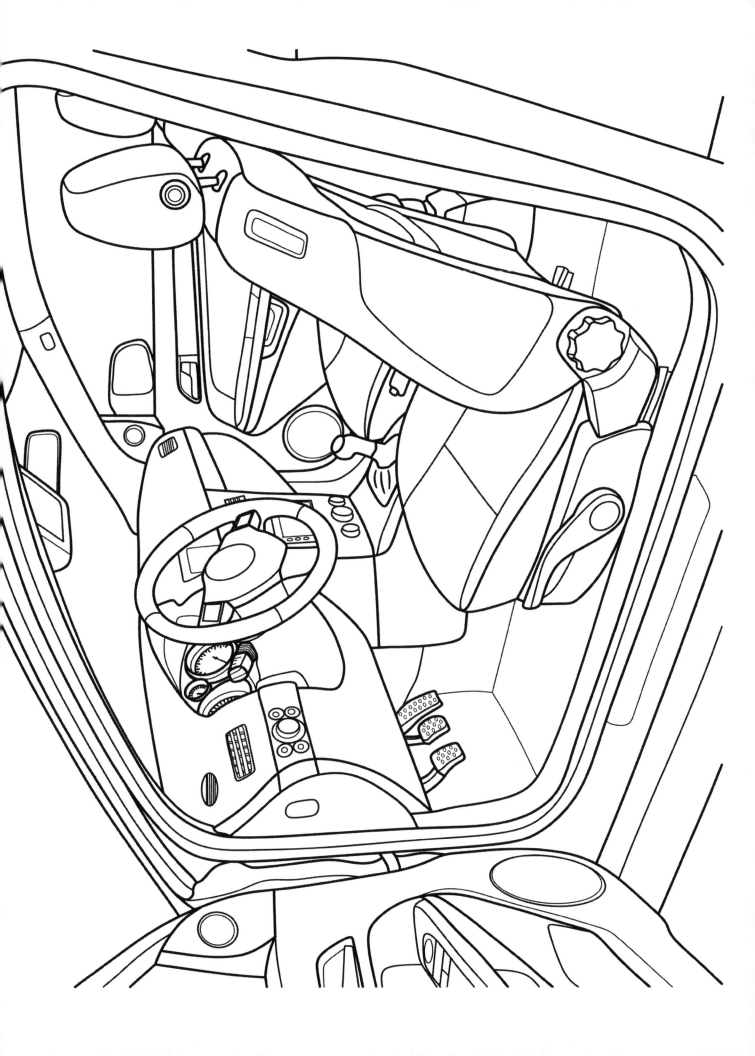

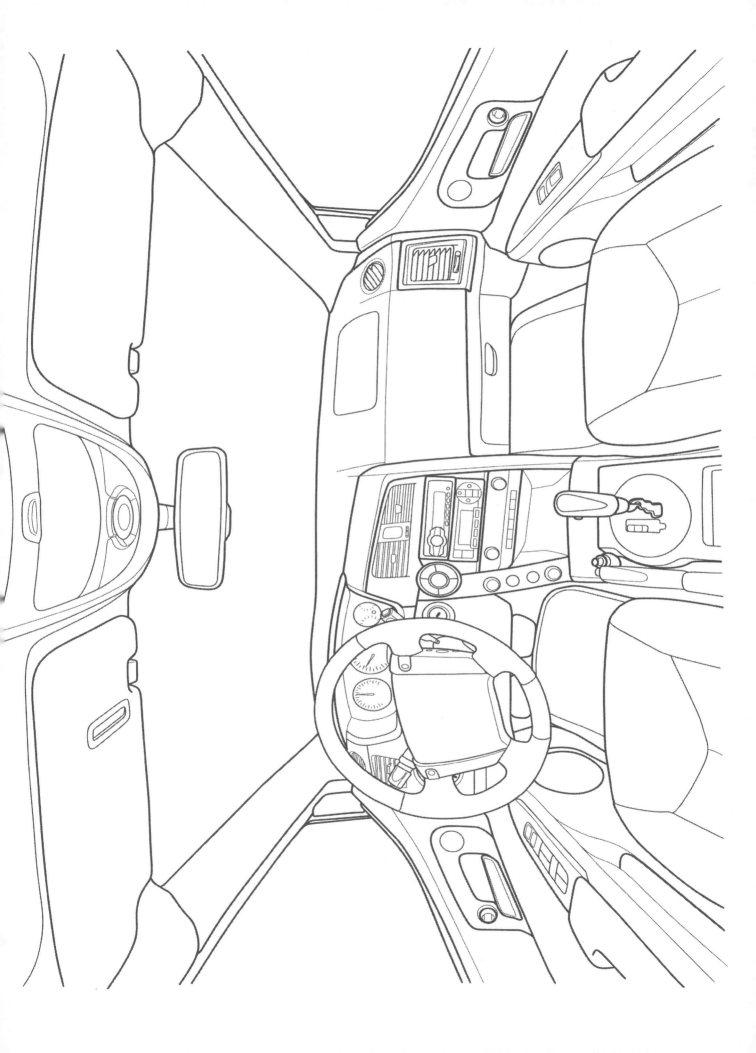

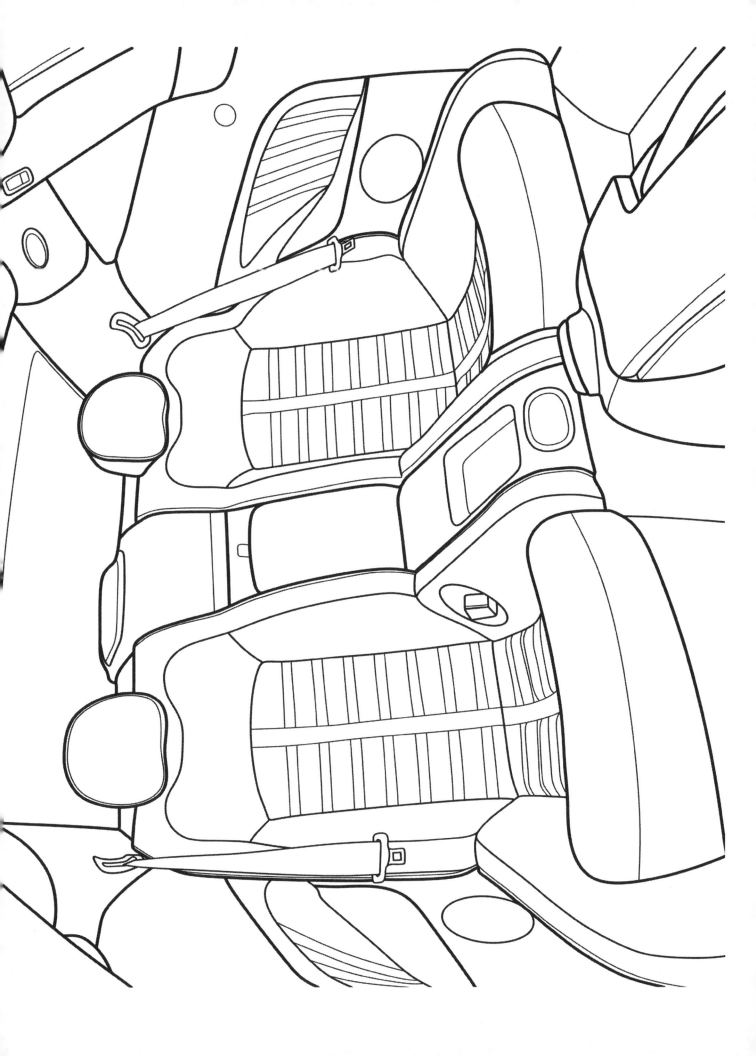

Made in United States
Orlando, FL
14 December 2024